What We Have in Common

A Brim Coloring Book

Written by Jane Landey
Edited by David Austin

Drawings by David Austin and Jane Austin

Published by CreateSpace: An Amazon Company.

Printed in U.S.A.

Introduction

What We Have in Common. Brim Coloring Books enable children to color the drawings as they read along! The books display the similarities of related animals. In this series, the duck and the pelican are compared. The facts enable children to appreciate common values. Thus, imbibing in them interest towards animals which could help them appreciate what they have in common with one another.

The Duck

And

The Pelican

The duck and the pelican have things in common. They are birds with big beaks. Both love to swim with their little ones.

A duck and a pelican meet on a lake.

Hello! I am a duck.

Hi! I am a pelican.

I have a pointed beak.

I have a longer beak!

And I can swim.

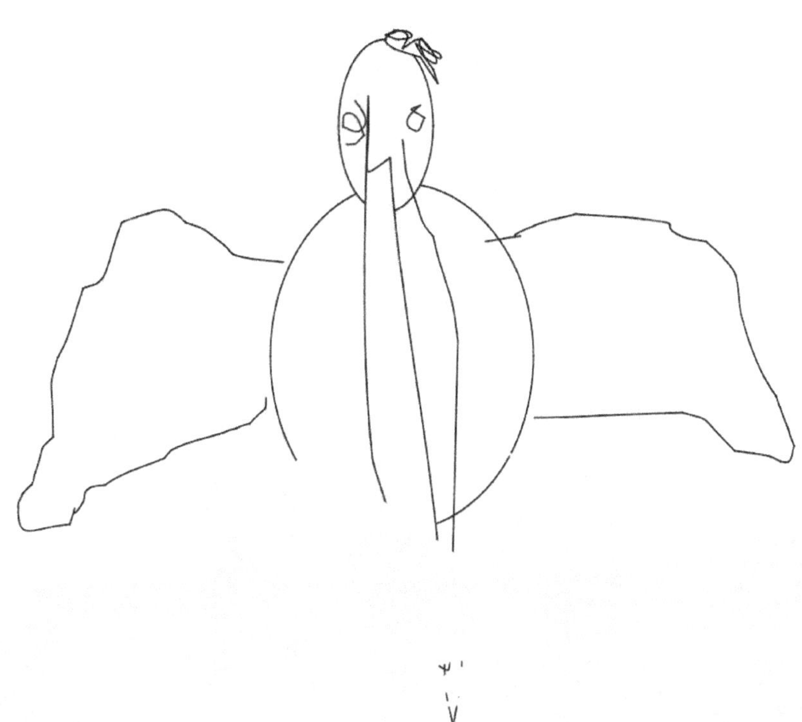

I can swim too!

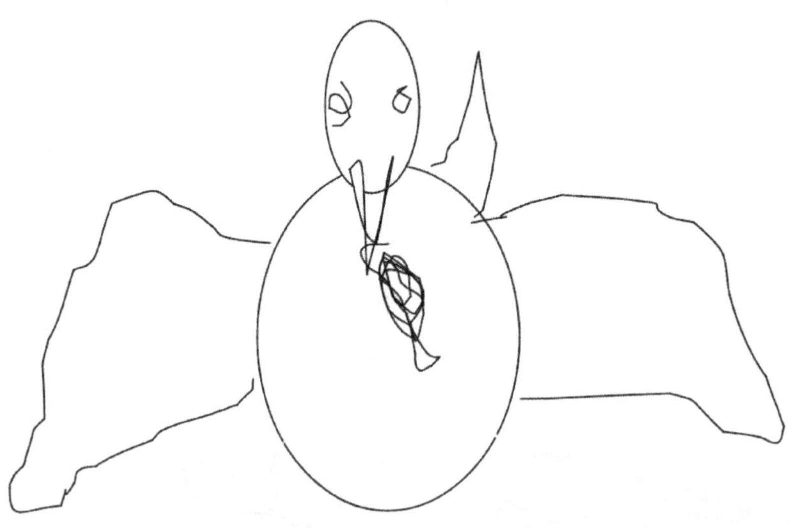

And I catch tiny fish.

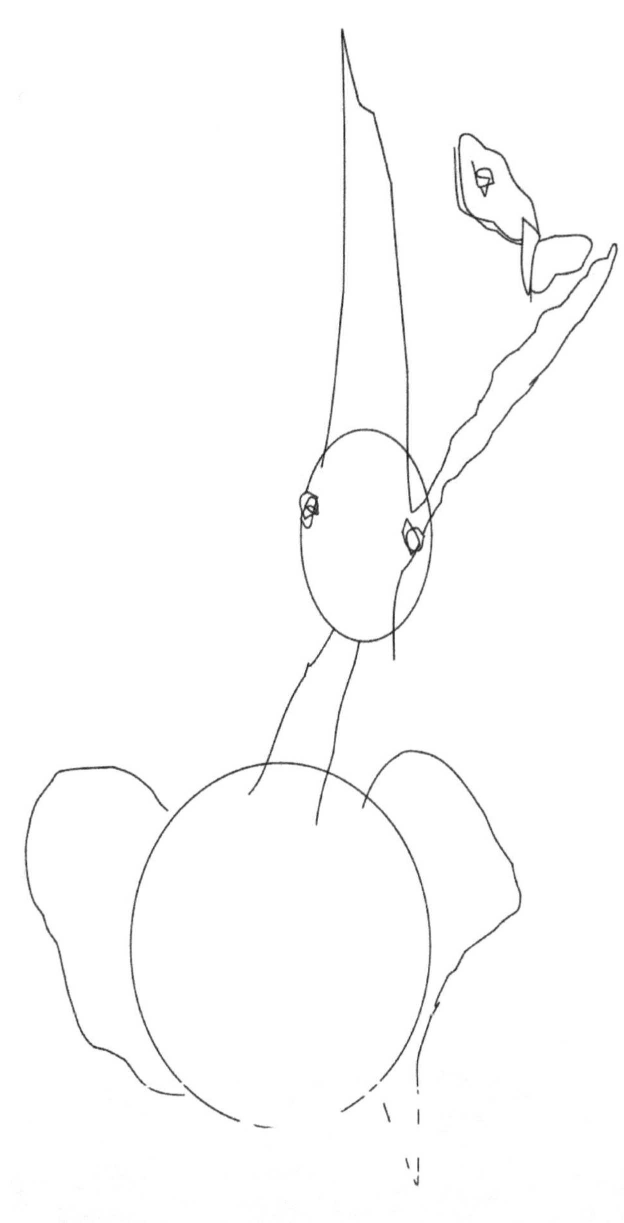

I catch fish too. Both tiny and big!

I search with my ducklings.

I travel in a flock!

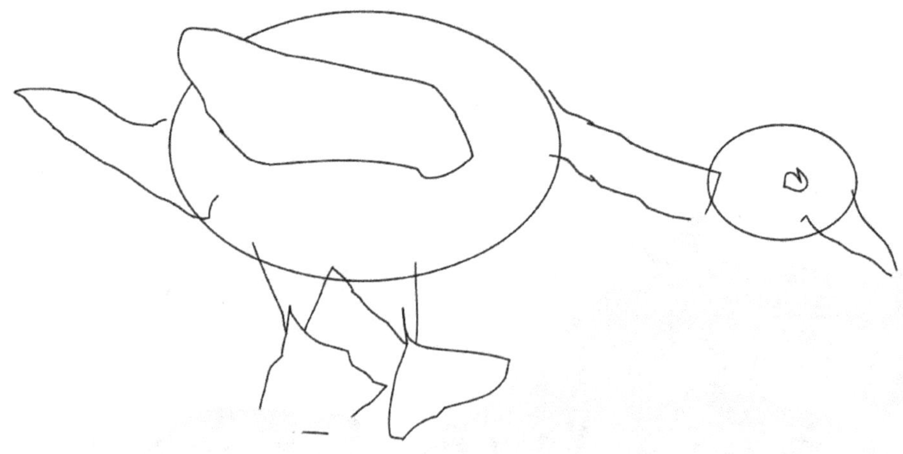

I can swallow water fast.

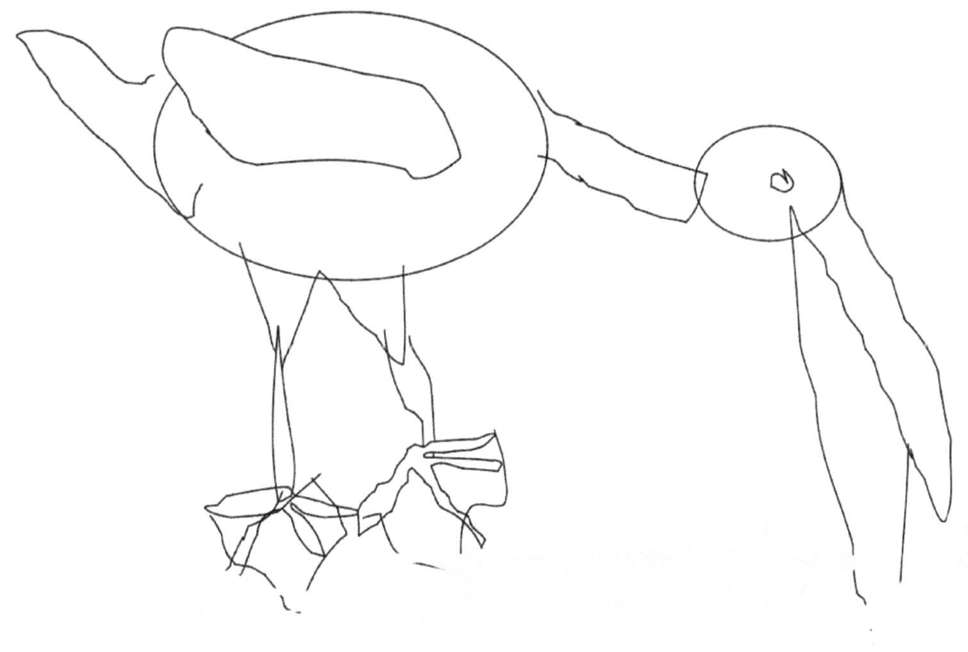

I can hold water in my bill!

I feed my young ones.

I feed my young ones too!

I lay eggs.

I lay eggs too!

My wings are long.

My wings are long too!

And I can fly.

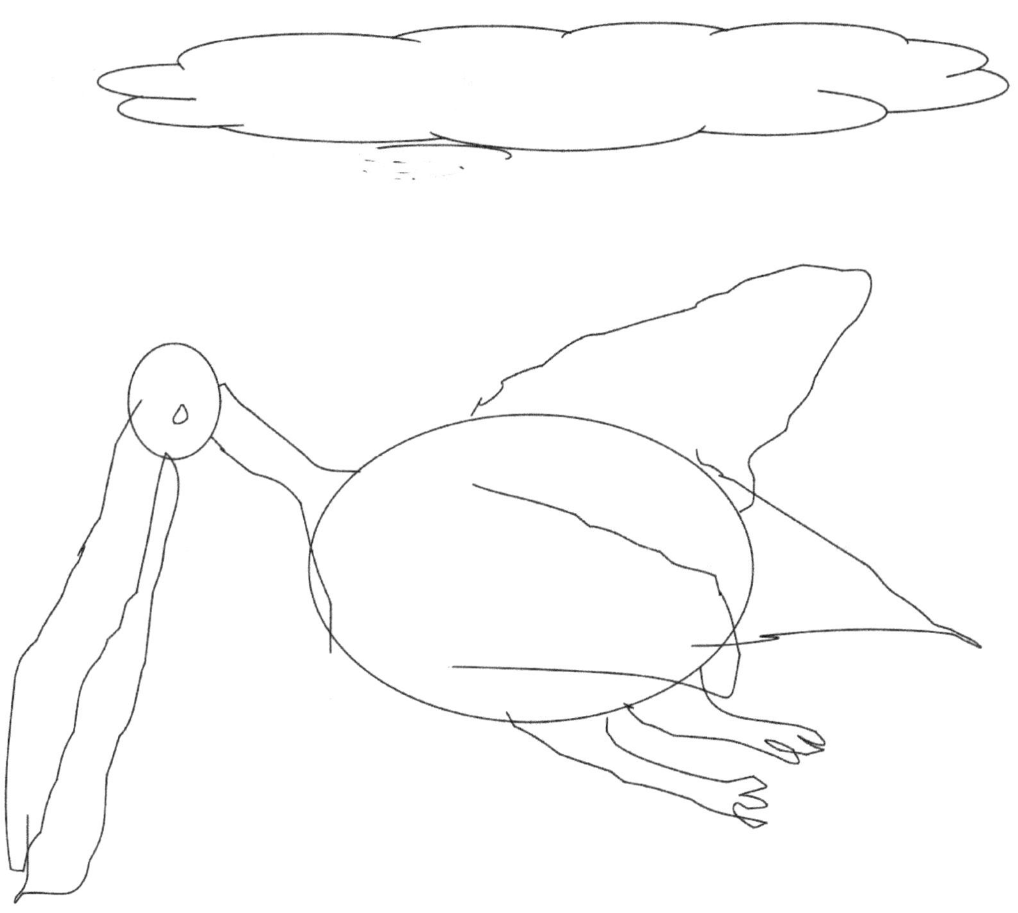

I can fly too!

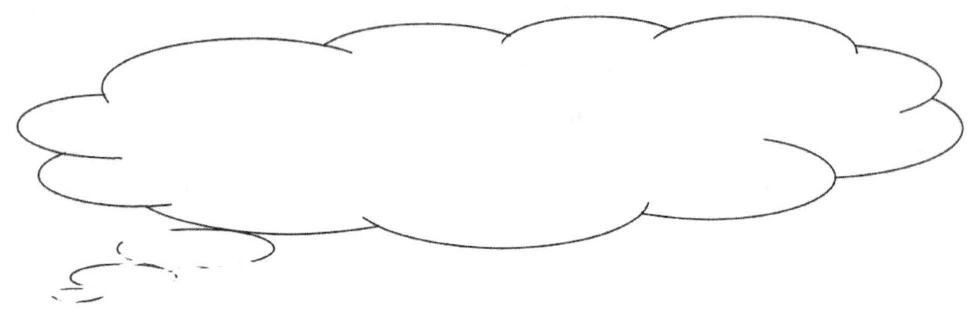

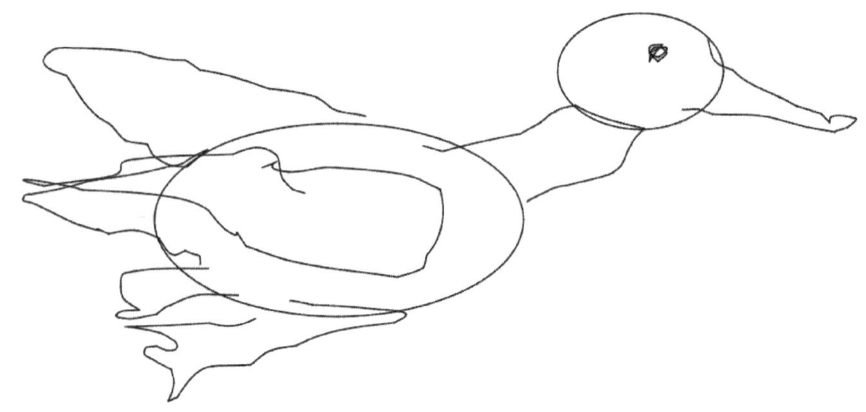

Off I go!

Off I go too!

I am walking.

I am walking too!

I play around the yard.

I play around the woods too!

Can I follow you to the woods?

Yes you can!

Hey, Let's go!

Alright!

Off we go!!

What We Have in Common Brim Coloring Books

Crocodile and Alligator
Turtle and Tortoise
Starfish and Octopus
Worm and Snake
Turkey and Vulture
Ostrich and Emu
Weka and Kiwi
Bat and Rat
Camel and Llama
Duck and Pelican
Kangaroo and Wallaby
Pig and Tapir
Skunk and Squirrel
Hedge and Anteater
Cat and Owl
Elephant and Rhinoceros
Dog and Fox
Buffalo and Bull
Leopard and Cheetah
Horse and Zebra